D0021237

SCIENCE PROJECT IDEAS

Science Project Ideas About

THE SUN

Robert Gardner

Enslow Publishers, Inc.

40 Industrial Road	PO Box 38
Box 398	Aldershot
Berkeley Heights, NJ 07922	Hants GU12 6BP
USA	UK

http://www.enslow.com

Library of Congress Cataloging-in-Publication Data

Gardner, Robert, 1929—
    Science project ideas about the sun / Robert Gardner.
       p. cm.—(Science project ideas)
    Includes bibliographical references and index.
    Summary: Uses experiments to illustrate the phases and patterns of the
sun as well as the reasons for its importance as an energy source.
    ISBN 0-89490-845-6
    1. Sun—Experiments—Juvenile literature. [1. Sun—Experiments.
2. Experiments.] I. Title. II. Series: Gardner, Robert, 1929–
Science project ideas.
QB521.5.G37 1997
523.7'078—DC20
                                        96-42693
                                            CIP
                                            AC

Printed in the United States of America

10 9 8 7 6 5 4

Illustration Credits: Jacob Katari

Photo Credits: Robert Gardner pp. 24, 25, 32, 38, 93; David Webster
p. 24 (a).

Cover Photo: Jerry McCrea

CONTENTS

INTRODUCTION

This book is made up of experiments about one of the most essential parts of nature—the sun. The experiments in this book use simple everyday materials you can find at home or at school.

These experiments will help you to work the way real scientists do. You will be answering questions by doing experiments to understand basic scientific principles. Most of the experiments provide detailed guidance, but some of them will raise questions and ask you to make up you own experiments to answer them. This is the kind of experiment that could be a particularly good start for a science fair project. Such experiments are marked with an asterisk (*).

Because sunshine in normal amounts is perfectly safe, the main ingredient of the investigations found in this book is not dangerous. However, you must observe one very important safety rule: **NEVER LOOK DIRECTLY AT THE SUN!** *The sun is so bright that it can cause serious damage to your eyes. Also, prolonged exposure to the sun can cause skin cancer.*

Please note: **If an experiment uses anything that has a potential for danger, you will be asked to work with an adult.** *Please do so! The purpose of this teamwork is to prevent you from being hurt.*

Science Project Ideas About the Sun *invites you to step outside on sunny days and carry out experiments that will help you learn more about the sun and how science is done.*

MEASUREMENT ABBREVIATIONS			
centimeter	cm	**mile**	mi
cubic centimeter	cu cm	**milliliter**	ml
kilogram	kg	**ounce**	oz
kilometer	km	**second**	sec
meter	m	**square centimeter**	sq cm

Finally we shall place the Sun himself at the center of the Universe.

(Nicholas Copernicus)

1

THE SUN: OUR OWN STAR

Did you know that we have our very own star? That star is the sun. Because the sun appears to be so much bigger than all the other stars we see, we normally don't think of it as a star. But it is! It looks much bigger than other stars because it is so close to us. It is only 150 million kilometers (93 million miles) from the earth.

Now that you know how far away the sun is, you may not think it is very close. To travel that far, you would have to circle the earth 3,750 times. Even the light from the sun takes 8 minutes and 20 seconds to reach the earth. But compared to other stars, it is not far away at all. To get to the next closest star, you would have to travel 40 trillion kilometers (40,000,000,000,000 km) or 25 trillion miles. Even if you could travel at the speed of light, it would take you more than four years to reach that star.

The sun is much bigger than the earth. The earth's diameter (the distance from one side to the other through the center) is approximately 13,000 km (8,000 mi). The sun's diameter is 1.4 million kilometers (870,000 mi). So the sun's diameter and circumference (girth or distance around) is 109 times bigger than the earth's. But its volume is 1,300,000 times greater than the earth's. Do you see why? (If you don't, you will after you do Experiment 1.1 later in this chapter.)

The sun is much hotter than the earth. While the average temperature on the earth's surface is 20°C (68°F), the sun's surface temperature is 5,500°C (9,900°F). At the sun's center, the temperature is about 16,000,000°C

(29,000,000°F). However, at the earth's core, the temperature is only 6,500°C (12,000°F).

The sun is 330,000 times as massive as the earth. The sun's mass is nearly two million trillion trillion kilograms (a 2 followed by 30 zeros) or two thousand trillion trillion tons. The earth is only six trillion trillion kilograms (a 6 followed by 24 zeros). It is the sun's huge mass that gives it the gravitational force needed to make all the planets revolve around it.

The matter that makes up the sun is mostly hydrogen (75 percent) and helium (24 percent). The remaining 1 percent is made up of the other elements. Nuclear reactions go on within the sun. These reactions produce the vast energy the sun emits each second. The 400 trillion trillion watts of power the sun releases provides its luminosity, which is a measure of its brightness. The sun produces a lot of energy, but many stars produce more and are much more luminous. Sirius, the brightest star in our sky, is 23 times brighter than our sun. Other stars are thousands of times brighter than the sun, but some of them are so far away that they cannot be seen without a telescope.

The earth's orbit about the sun is not a perfect circle. It is slightly elliptical (oval). The elliptical nature of the earth's orbit is very

FIGURE 1

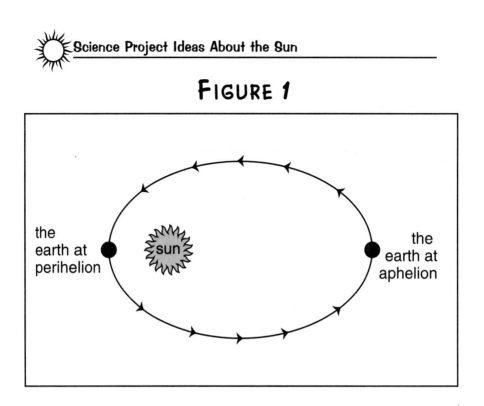

The earth's elliptical orbit about the sun is shown. The elliptical nature of the orbit is greatly exaggerated; it is really almost a circle.

much exaggerated in Figure 1. This is done to show that the distance between the earth and sun does change. The earth is at perihelion (closest to the sun) in early January when it is about 147 million kilometers (92 million miles) from the sun. It is at aphelion (farthest from the sun) in early July when the sun is about 152 million kilometers (95 million miles) from the earth. As you can see, our distance from the sun does not change very much. But you may wonder how we can be closest to the sun in winter and farthest from the sun in summer. If you lived south of the equator where the seasons are reversed, you probably would not wonder about this fact. (See Experiment 1.2 later in this chapter.)

Earth's average speed along its orbit about the sun is 29.8 km/sec or 18.6 mi/sec. Its speed is slightly greater when it is closer to the sun and slightly less when it is farther from the sun. Therefore, the earth moves slightly faster around the sun in the winter and a bit more slowly in the summer. (See Experiment 1.3 later in this chapter.)

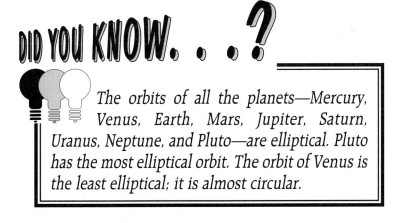

DID YOU KNOW. . . ?

The orbits of all the planets—Mercury, Venus, Earth, Mars, Jupiter, Saturn, Uranus, Neptune, and Pluto—are elliptical. Pluto has the most elliptical orbit. The orbit of Venus is the least elliptical; it is almost circular.

Experiment *1.1

THE SUN AND EARTH: DIAMETER AND VOLUME

To do this experiment you will need:

✔ clay	✔ ruler

You know that the sun's diameter and girth are 109 times bigger than the earth's. Yet, its volume is more than a million times greater. To see why this is true, you can begin by making a cube from clay. A cube is a block that has the same length, width, and height. Using the clay and ruler, make a cube that is 1 cm on each side, as shown in Figure 2. How many faces does the cube have?

The area of the surface of each face is found by multiplying the length of the face by its width (its length times its width). If the length and width are measured in centimeters, the area will be in square centimeters (sq cm). As you can see, the surface area of one face of the cube you have made is:

$$\text{1 cm x 1 cm = 1 sq cm or 1 cm}^2$$

FIGURE 2

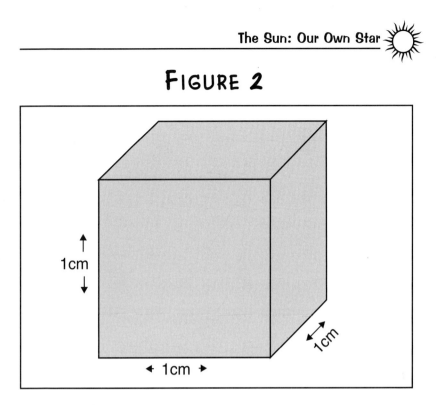

A cube of clay 1 centimeter (cm) on a side is shown.

What is the total area of all the cube's six faces?

The volume of the cube you have made is the space that it occupies. Space has three dimensions: length, width, and height. The volume of any cube can be found by multiplying its length by its width by its height (volume = length x width x height). The volume of your cube will be in cubic centimeters (cu cm). The cube you have made is 1 cm long, 1 cm wide, and 1 cm high. Therefore, the volume of the cube you made is:

💡 1 cm x 1 cm x 1 cm = 1 cu cm or 1 cm^3

Now make a second cube of clay. Make this one 2 cm wide, 2 cm long, and 2 cm high. Place the second cube beside the first. (1) How many of the small cubes would you need to put together to have a face with the same area as one face of the larger cube? (2) What is the area, in square centimeters, of each face of the larger cube? (3) What is the total area of all the cube's six faces? (4) How does the total area of this cube compare with the total area of the first cube?

Again, place the first cube beside the second one. (5) How many times would the small cube fit into the larger cube?

Multiply the length of the larger cube by its width and height. (6) How many cubic centimeters are occupied by the larger cube? (7) How does the volume you found in question 6 compare with the volume of the larger cube that you found in question 5? You can check your answers to questions 1 through 7 by turning to page 93 in the back of the book.

Now let's return to the question about the sun's diameter and volume as compared with the earth's. Think of the earth as a cube. Think

FIGURE 3

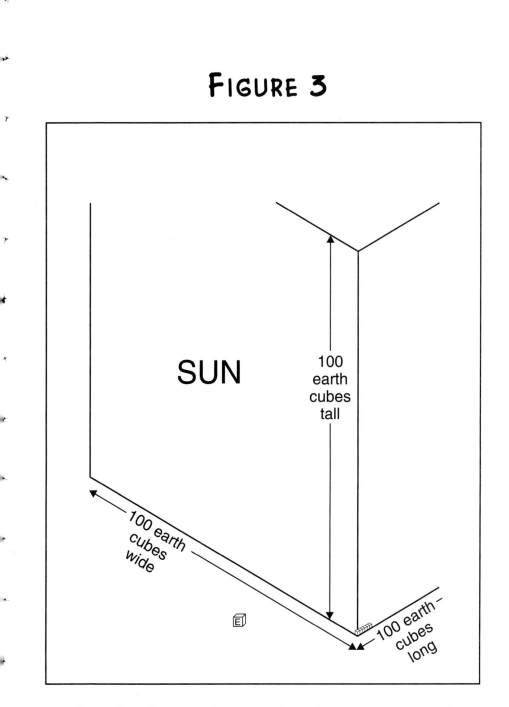

The earth and sun are shown as cubes. The sun is approximately 100 times as long, wide, and tall as the earth.

of the sun as a cube that is 100 times as wide. As you can see from Figure 3, you could place 100 earth's along each edge of the sun. Then you would have to stack 100 rows of 100 earths before you covered one face of the sun. Finally, you would have to make 100 more such stacks before you had a cube as thick as the sun. All together, you have had to use 100 x 100 x 100 earth cubes to make a cube the size of the sun. How many earth cubes will fit into the sun cube?

The sun is actually 109 times the diameter of the earth. If you multiply 109 x 109 x 109, you will find that it is just about 1,300,000 (1.3 million). That is why the sun's volume is 1,300,000 times greater than the earth's, even though its diameter is only 109 times bigger than the earth's.

DID YOU KNOW. . .?

The diameter of Jupiter is about 11 times as large as the earth's diameter. That means the earth would fit into Jupiter about 1,300 times (11 x 11 x 11).

A More Distant Sun and Summer's Heat

To do this experiment you will need:

✔ flashlight   ✔ globe

Those of us who live in the northern hemisphere are closer to the sun in winter than we are in summer. You may have wondered how it can be colder in the winter when we are closer to the sun. To see how this is possible, shine a flashlight on a globe. Hold the flashlight so its circular beam points directly onto the Tropic of Capricorn. The Tropic of Capricorn is a line on the globe that runs around the Earth 23.5 degrees south of the equator. On the first day of winter, the sun appears to follow a path that is directly over the Tropic of Capricorn. Now move the flashlight upward without changing its tilt (the direction of its beam) until its light falls on the United States. The beam should be parallel to its original direction (pointing in the same direction as before), as shown in Figure 4. It now shines on a more northern part of the globe. (Since the sun is so far away, rays of sunlight reaching the earth are very nearly parallel.) As you can see, the flashlight beam shining on the United States no longer makes a circular pattern of light. The beam is now spread out over a much broader surface.

Because the same amount of sunlight is spread over a bigger surface, the sunlight is less intense. The same energy is spread over a much bigger area. Winter sunlight that shines directly on points south of the equator, strikes the northern hemisphere at a steep angle. The less intense sunlight in northern regions gives

FIGURE 4

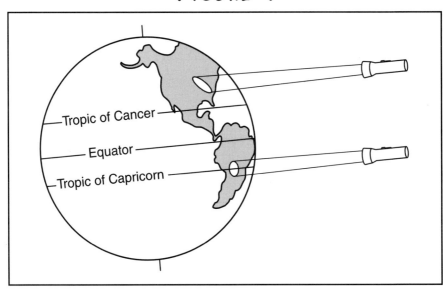

The winter sun is directly over the Tropic of Capricorn on about December 20. The sunlight striking the United States at that time is spread over a larger area and so is less intense.

us less energy to heat that part of the earth. As a result, temperatures in the northern hemisphere are lower during winter months.

Continue to move the flashlight farther north along the globe without changing the direction of its beam. You will find that no light reaches the north pole. It remains dark throughout the winter.

Now move the flashlight so that it points directly at the Tropic of Cancer. The Tropic of Cancer is a line on the globe that runs around the earth 23.5 degrees north of the equator. On the first day of summer, the sun appears to follow a path that is directly over the Tropic of Cancer.

Move the flashlight slowly northward on the globe without changing the beam's direction until its light falls on the United States. The beam should be parallel to its original direction, but slightly farther north on the globe. As you can see, the beam shining on the United States makes a nearly circular pattern of light. The same light is spread over much less area than it was when the winter sun (flashlight) was pointed at the Tropic of Capricorn. The more intense summer sunlight provides more warmth, raising temperatures in the northern hemisphere. What will happen in the southern hemisphere during our summer?

Experiment 1.3

THE EARTH'S SPEED IN ITS ORBIT

To do this experiment you will need:

- ✔ good calandar or a calandar and almanac
- ✔ pencil and paper or a pocket calculator

Earlier, you learned that the earth's speed along its orbit is slightly greater when it is closer to the sun and slightly less when it is farther from the sun. Therefore, the earth should move slightly faster around the sun in the winter and a bit more slowly in the summer.

If this is true, summer should last slightly longer than winter in the northern hemisphere. To check up on this, count the number of days from the beginning of winter to the beginning of spring on a calendar that provides this information. (If the calendar does not tell when winter and spring begin, an almanac will.) Then count the number of days from the beginning of summer to the beginning of autumn. Is summer slightly longer than winter? If so, how much longer is it?

Yesternight the sun went hence,
And yet is here today.

(John Donne)

2

Sun and Shadows

Do you think a shadow can be made if the sun is not shining? After all, you can see your shadow in moonlight. However, moonlight is really sunlight that is reflected from the moon to the earth. So it is correct to say that there will be no shadows without the sun, even if we take moonlight into account. The only other natural light that can cast a shadow on the earth is light from the planet Venus. But the light from Venus is also reflected sunlight. Unless we consider artificial light such as electric lightbulbs, oil lamps, and candles, we need the sun to create a shadow. Can we say that shadows cast by lightning depend on the sun?

A shadow is created whenever an object prevents sunlight, or other light, from reaching the space behind the object. Since there are lots of objects on the earth, we can expect to see lots of shadows. Look for them. They are everywhere! In this chapter we will concentrate on just a few of them. The first one is your own shadow.

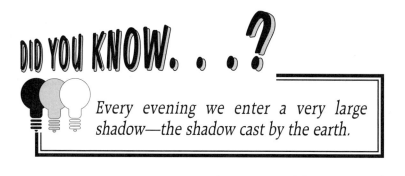

DID YOU KNOW. . .?

Every evening we enter a very large shadow—the shadow cast by the earth.

Experiment 2.1

YOU AND YOUR SHADOW

To do this experiment you will need:

✔ sunny day	✔ a friend

Go outside on a sunny day shortly after the sun comes up. Remember: **NEVER LOOK DIRECTLY AT THE SUN. IT CAN DAMAGE YOUR EYES!** How long is your shadow? What happens to the length of your shadow as noon approaches? At what time of day is your shadow shortest? What happens to the length of your shadow as evening approaches? Can you explain why your shadow changes during the course of a day?

How is your shadow shortly after sunrise like your shadow shortly before sunset? How are your shadows different at these two times?

Can you hide your shadow in another shadow? How can you separate from your shadow? Can you and a friend do a shadow handshake without your hands actually touching?

Experiment *2.2

OBJECTS, SUN, AND SHADOWS

To do this experiment you will need:

- ✔ sunny day
- ✔ heavy cardboard
- ✔ tin can
- ✔ ball
- ✔ small box
- ✔ cone-shaped object such as an ice cream cone
- ✔ pyramid-shaped object
- ✔ scissors
- ✔ light cardboard

Support a sheet of heavy cardboard so that it faces the sun, as shown in Figure 5. Hold a tin can in front of the heavy cardboard. How can you turn the can so that it casts a circular shadow on the cardboard? How can you turn the can so that it casts a rectangular shadow (one with straight sides and right angles like the sides of a box)?

Can you use a ball to cast a rectangular shadow on the cardboard? How many shadows with different shapes can you cast using (a) a ball, (b) a small box, (c) a cone-shaped object, (d) a pyramid-shaped object?

FIGURE 5

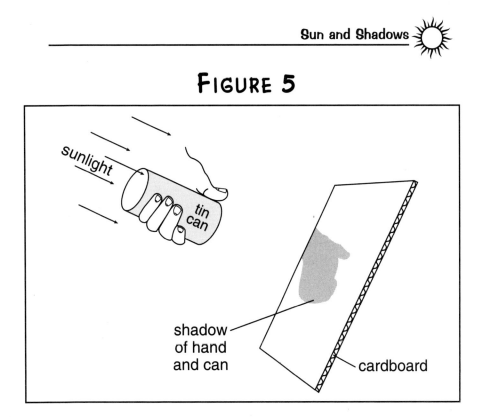

A tin can held in sunlight will cast a shadow on a piece of cardboard. Is it possible to make the can cast a rectangular shadow?

Using scissors, cut a square, a rectangle, a circle, and an ellipse (oval) from a sheet of thin cardboard. Can you cast a square shadow using the rectangular-shaped cardboard? Can you cast a rectangular shadow with the square cardboard? Can you cast an oval shadow using the cardboard circle? Can you cast a circular shadow with the oval cardboard? What other shadow shapes can you make with these four pieces of cardboard?

Mystery Shadows

The shadows shown in the following photographs were cast by things in sunlight. Try to guess what made each of the shadows shown. After you've made your predictions, turn to the answers on page 93 to see if you were right.

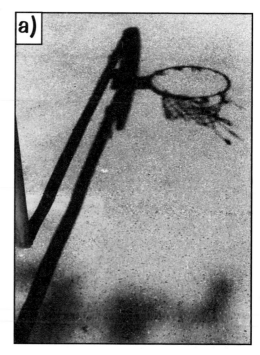

a)

b)

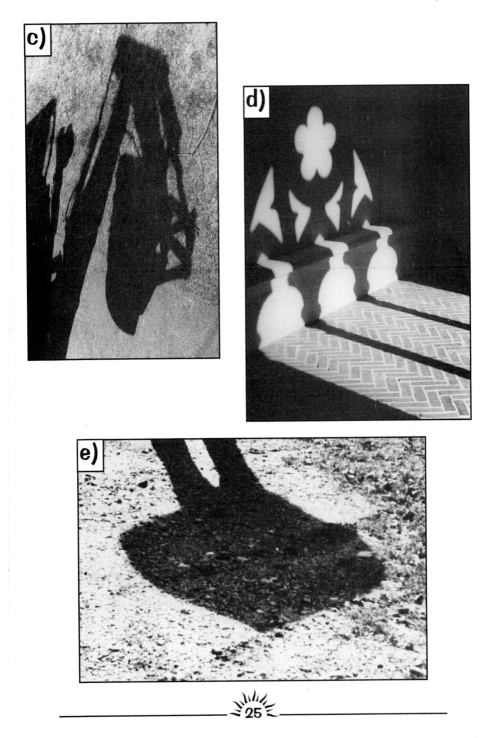

Experiment *2.3

SHADOWS THAT GROW AND SHADOWS THAT DON'T GROW

To do this experiment you will need:

- ✔ lamp socket
- ✔ clear lightbulb with a straight filament
- ✔ white wall
- ✔ common pins
- ✔ sheet of cardboard
- ✔ small plate or pan
- ✔ pencil

Place a lamp about 2 m (6 ft) from a white wall in a darkened room. The lamp's socket should hold a clear lightbulb that has a straight filament. Turn the lamp so the lightbulb's straight filament is perpendicular to the wall (pointed at the wall), as shown in Figure 6. If you look at the glowing lightbulb from the wall, the end of the filament looks like a point of light. Hold your hand close to the wall. How does the size of your hand's shadow compare with the size of your hand? What happens to the size of the shadow as you move your hand closer to the point of light? Can you explain why the shadow's size changes?

FIGURE 6

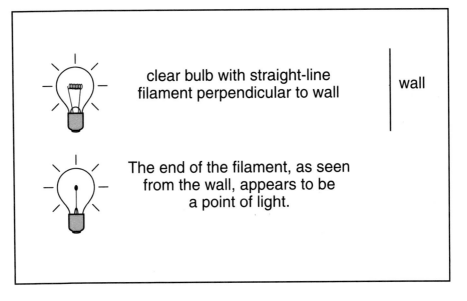

clear bulb with straight-line
filament perpendicular to wall

wall

The end of the filament, as seen
from the wall, appears to be
a point of light.

The end of a clear bulb's straight-line filament is seen as a point
of light from the wall.

Think of the light coming from the filament
as rays that extend straight outward in all
directions. (After all, why should light prefer
one direction to another?) To see that light
really does travel as shown in Figure 7, stick
three common pins in a line at one end of a
sheet of cardboard. The pins should be about
1 cm (0.5 in) apart. Hold the side of the
cardboard with the pins near the end of the
lightbulb's filament. Look at the shadows cast
by the pins. How do these shadows show that

light really does travel outward in different directions from the end of the filament? How does this experiment help you to explain why the shadow of your hand grew larger as you moved it toward the lightbulb?

What do you predict will happen to the directions of the pin's shadows as you move the pins farther from the light? Try it. Were you right? How does this help you to explain why the sun's light rays are nearly parallel when they reach the earth?

FIGURE 7

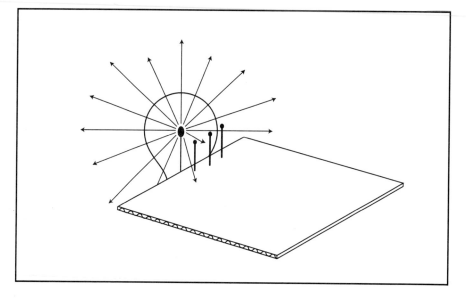

Light is emitted in all directions from a point of light. How can the shadows of the pins stuck in a cardboard sheet show that light really does travel outward in all directions?

Take a sheet of cardboard outside into the sunshine. Turn the cardboard so that it faces the sun. Hold your hand in front of the cardboard. The shadow of your hand should fall on the cardboard. Slowly move your hand away from the cardboard. Notice that the size of your hand's shadow does not change. What does this tell you about the rays of light reaching the earth from the sun?

Stick three common pins in a line at one end of a sheet of cardboard as you did before. Hold the cardboard so that the end with the pins is toward the sun. Look at the shadows cast by the pins. **NEVER LOOK AT THE SUN. IT CAN DAMAGE YOUR EYES!** What do these shadows tell you about the light rays that reach the earth from the sun?

Place a small circular plate or pan on the sheet of cardboard. Use a pencil and the plate or pan to draw a circle on the cardboard. Stick about eight common pins into the cardboard along the pencil line that marks the outline (circumference) of the circle you have drawn (see Figure 8). Predict the direction of the shadow that each pin will cast when you hold the circle of pins in bright sunlight.

Take the circle of pins inside. Turn on the clear lightbulb that you used before. Predict the direction of the shadow that each pin in

FIGURE 8

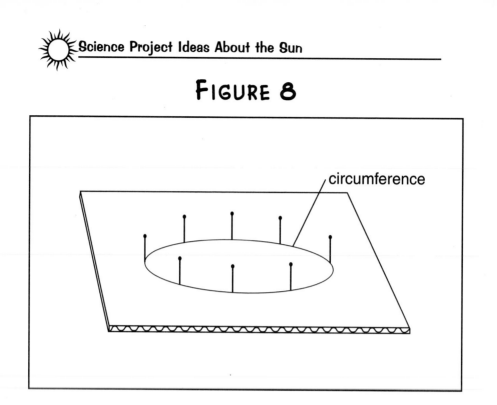

Pins are placed along the circumference (outline) of a circle drawn on a sheet of cardboard. What will be true of the direction of each pin's shadow when the sheet is held in sunlight?

the circle will cast when you hold them close to the point of light. Then try the experiment. Were your predictions correct? Predict what will happen to the directions of the pins' shadows when you move the cardboard farther from the point of light? Try it! Were you right?

Experiment *2.4

SUN DAPPLES

To do this experiment you will need:

- ✔ sunny day
- ✔ leafy tree
- ✔ two file cards
- ✔ pin
- ✔ pegboard

On a bright sunny day find a leafy tree that provides lots of shade. If you look under the tree, you will see many small circles like the ones in the photograph shown in Figure 9. These circles are called sun dapples.

To see what causes the sun dapples, you will need two file cards and a pin. Use the pin to make a small hole through the center of one of the file cards. Hold both cards in sunlight, as shown in Figure 10. **NEVER LOOK AT THE SUN. IT CAN DAMAGE YOUR EYES!** The card with the pinhole in it should be between the sun and the other file card. Look at the lower card carefully. It serves as a screen on which you can see an image of the sun. What happens to the size of the image if

FIGURE 9

The round spots of light in the above photograph of the shadow of a tree are images of the sun.

you move the screen farther from the pinhole? What do you think will happen to the size of the sun's image if you move the screen closer to the pinhole? Try it! Were you right?

Next, use the pin to make a second pinhole in the upper card. How many images of the sun do you see on the screen now? How many images of the sun do you expect to see if you make a third pinhole in the card? How many do you see?

FIGURE 10

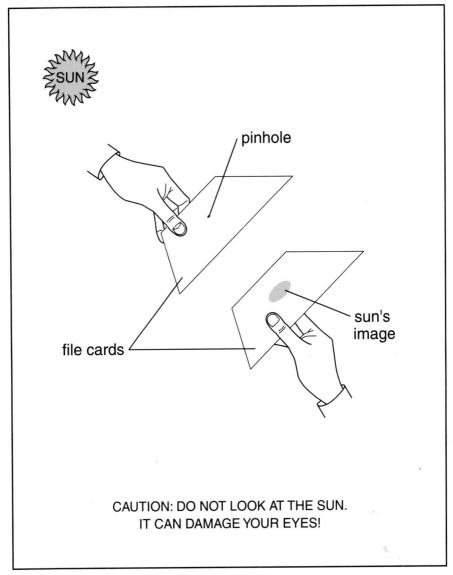

A pinhole in a card nearer the sun forms an image of the sun on a card held beneath it.

Make a large number of pinholes in the upper card. How many images of the sun do you see on the screen? You have made your own set of sun dapples.

Hold a piece of pegboard in sunlight. Look at the shadow of the pegboard. What do you think causes all the bright circles you see?

From what you have done and seen, how would you explain the sun dapples you saw under a shade tree?

DID YOU KNOW. . .?

Helium gas derives its name from the Greek word "helios," which means sun. The reason for this is that helium was first discovered on the sun, not on the earth. By analyzing the sun's light, scientists found spectral lines (certain colors) that were not emitted by any known elements. Later, helium was found on the earth. It is emitted by many radioactive elements.

Experiment *2.5

SHARP AND FUZZY SHADOWS

To do this experiment you will need:

- ✔ sunny day
- ✔ tall object such as a post or flagpole
- ✔ frosted lightbulb
- ✔ clear lightbulb with a straight filament
- ✔ pencil
- ✔ white wall
- ✔ lamp socket

Look at the shadow of a tall object such as a post or flagpole early in the morning or late in the afternoon. You can see that the shadow near the base of the post or pole is quite sharp. There is a clear line between the dark shadow and the bright sunlight on either side of the shadow. But the end of the shadow farthest from the pole is fuzzy. There is no sharp line separating the dark shadow from the bright sunlight. The outer part of the shadow is not as dark as the shadow near the base of the pole. Is the same thing true of your own shadow? Is the shadow of your legs sharp and dark, while the shadow of your head is fuzzy and lighter?

To find out why the near part of your shadow is sharp while the far end is fuzzy, you can do an experiment indoors. You will need an ordinary frosted lightbulb, a clear lightbulb with a straight filament like the one shown in Figure 6, a pencil, and a white wall. Place the clear bulb in a lamp socket a meter (several feet) from the white wall. Turn the bulb so that the end of the filament looks like a point of light when you stand near the wall. Hold a pencil between the point of light and the wall. You will see its sharp and very distinct shadow on the wall.

Turn off the light and let the bulb cool. When it has cooled, replace it with a frosted bulb. Turn the light on again. Hold the same pencil between the wall and the frosted bulb. You will see a shadow that is much fuzzier than the one you saw with the point of light.

Can you explain why the point of light makes a sharp shadow while the frosted bulb makes a fuzzier shadow? If you can, you can explain why your own morning shadow has a sharp and a fuzzy end. Remember, the sun is a round ball of light, more like a frosted bulb than a point of light. Light from one side of the sun falls on the shadow cast by light from the

FIGURE 11

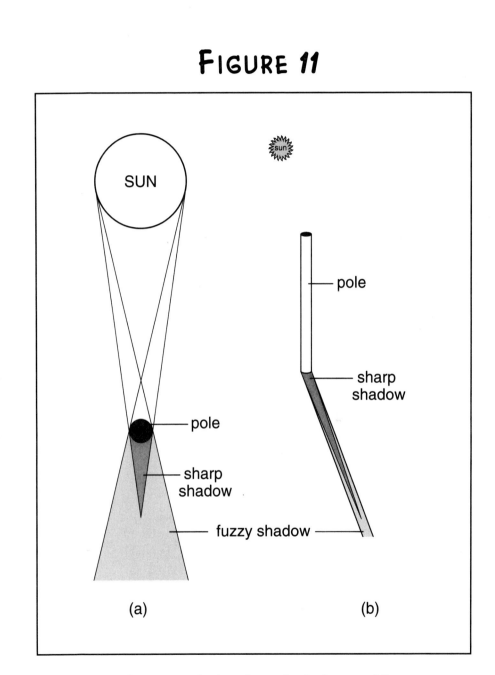

A pole casts a shadow that is both sharp and fuzzy.

a) The shadow is shown from above (not to scale).
b) The shadow is shown from the ground.

sun's other side and vice versa. A diagram of what happens is shown in Figure 11. Close to the pole, sunlight does not travel far enough to reach more than the shadow's edge. But farther from the pole, the light travels far enough to fall on the shadow cast by light from the opposite side of the sun.

Can you explain why the bottom part of the tennis net in the photograph in Figure 12 casts a sharp shadow on the court, while the shadow of the upper part is fuzzy?

FIGURE 12

At the top of this photograph, the bottom of a tennis net is shown touching the court. Notice how fuzzy the shadow of the top of the net is compared with the shadow of the bottom of the net.

Eclipses of the Sun and Moon

Just as you cast a shadow on the earth, so may the moon. The moon's shadow is seen when the moon comes between the sun and the earth (Figure 13a) during a new moon. It is called an eclipse of the sun (a solar eclipse) because the sun, or part of it, is hidden by the moon. Since the moon is much smaller than the sun, its shadow covers only a small part of the earth. And the moon's shadow, like yours, has a dark portion (umbra) and a fuzzy portion (penumbra). The umbra touches only a tiny part of the earth's surface, if any. Therefore, only a small area of the earth will lie in the darkest part of the shadow (the umbra). The dark part is where all of the sun's light is blocked by the moon. During a solar eclipse, the moon's umbra makes a narrow path as it moves across the earth's surface. The width of this shadow will never exceed 274 km (170 mi). Sometimes only the penumbra reaches the earth. When that happens, part of the sun is visible during the eclipse.

Of course, the earth can cast a shadow too. We enter its shadow every evening after sunset. And we emerge from its shadow every morning at sunrise. Sometimes we can see the earth's shadow on the moon. This is called a lunar

FIGURE 13

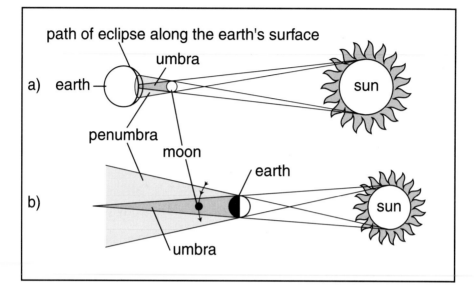

a) An eclipse of the sun (solar eclipse—not to scale) is shown.

b) An eclipse of the moon (lunar eclipse—not to scale) is shown.
The moon is shown passing through the earth's umbra.

eclipse because the moon becomes partially hidden by the earth's shadow. This can happen when the sun, earth, and a full moon all lie along the same line, as shown in Figure 13b. Because the earth's atmosphere bends some sunlight around the earth, our view of the moon is never totally blocked by the earth's shadow. Even if the moon enters the dark umbra of the earth's shadow, some sunlight reaches the moon. The moon darkens and takes on a copper color, but it doesn't disappear the way the sun does during a total eclipse.

There are at least two, but never more than five, solar eclipses each year. Lunar eclipses occur just about as often. However, the most eclipses, both solar and lunar, that can occur in one year is seven. You might wonder why we don't have solar and lunar eclipses every month, since full and new moons occur monthly. The reason is that the moon's orbit is not exactly on the same plane as the earth's orbit about the sun. As a result, the sun, moon, and earth are seldom lined up exactly with one another.

It is always safe to view an eclipse of the moon because the light from the moon is quite dim. But **NEVER LOOK AT THE SUN!** Even during an eclipse the sun is so bright it can cause severe damage to your eyes. One way to view a solar eclipse is to look at a pinhole image of the sun. Make a pinhole in one side of a large cardboard box. Turn the box so the pinhole faces the sun. With your back to the sun, place the box over your head. You can view the sun's image on a sheet of white paper taped to the inside wall of the box opposite the pinhole. Sunlight entering the box through the pinhole will form an image on the white paper. If you use a pegboard, you can see a lot of images of the sun. You might call them eclipsed sun dapples.

A Model of a Solar Eclipse

To do this experiment you will need:

- ✔ frosted lightbulb in socket
- ✔ penny or another coin
- ✔ scissors
- ✔ drinking straw
- ✔ file card or paper pad

It's easy to make a model of a solar eclipse. Use an ordinary frosted lightbulb to represent the sun. A penny or another coin can represent the moon. Use scissors to make a slit about 0.6 cm (0.25 in) long in one end of a drinking straw, as shown in Figure 14a. The slit in the end of the straw will hold the coin. The straw serves as a handle.

Your head can represent the earth. Your eye can represent a place on the earth where the eclipse can be seen. Stand several feet from the glowing lightbulb. Hold the coin in front of one eye and move it until it blacks out part or all of the lightbulb (see Figure 14b). The coin's shadow falls on your eye and blocks your view of at least part of the bulb. In the same way,

FIGURE 14

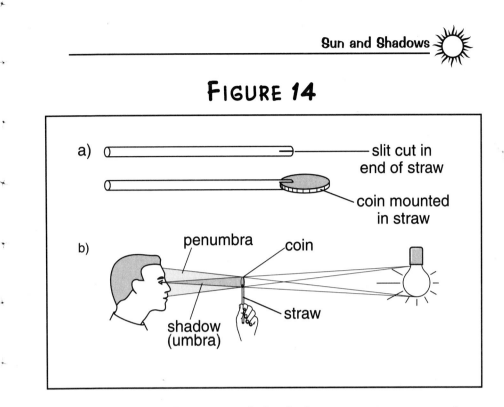

a) Make a small slit in one end of a drinking straw. Mount a small coin in the straw.

b) The coin, which corresponds to the moon, casts a shadow on your eye. The lightbulb represents the sun; your eye represents the earth.

the moon during a solar eclipse casts a shadow on the earth and blocks out at least a part of the sun. **DO NOT DO THIS EXPERIMENT OUTDOORS WITH THE SUN!**

Move the coin closer to your eye. Does it block out more or less of the bulb as it moves closer to your eye? Slowly move the coin farther from your eye. Does the coin block out more or less of the bulb as you move it away?

Hold the coin far enough away so that it blocks the center part of the lightbulb but leaves a ring of light around the edge. This is what happens during what is called an annular eclipse. In an annular eclipse, a thin ring of light is still visible all around the edge of the sun.

You can also move the coin so that it blocks out the top, bottom, or one side of the lightbulb. This is what happens during a partial eclipse when the sun and moon are not quite in line with your location on the earth. As you might guess, you are more likely to see a partial eclipse than a total eclipse.

Take yourself out of the model by using a file card or a paper pad to represent the earth's surface. Hold the card or pad about 1 m (3 ft) from the glowing lightbulb. Then bring the coin near the lightbulb so you see its dark shadow (umbra) on the paper. Now slowly move the coin (moon) away from the paper (earth's surface). You will see the dark umbra grow smaller, while the fuzzy penumbra that surrounds it grows larger. At a certain point, the umbra disappears and only the fuzzy penumbra remains. This corresponds to an annular eclipse. During an annular eclipse, even if you are at the center of the moon's shadow, you can see a ring of light around the sun's blacked-out center.

Experiment *2.7

A MODEL OF A LUNAR ECLIPSE

To do this experiment you will need:

- ✔ Styrofoam or other soft, opaque spheres; one 5 cm (2 in) in diameter, the other 1.2–1.3 cm (0.5 in) in diameter
- ✔ stick 1.5 m (5 ft) long
- ✔ two small finishing nails
- ✔ tape
- ✔ sunlight

To make a model of a lunar eclipse you will need a Styrofoam ball with a diameter of 5 cm (2 in) and another with a diameter of 1.2–1.3 cm (0.5 in). You will also need a stick 1.5 m (5 ft) long and two small finishing nails that you can tape to each end of the stick, as shown in Figure 15. The large ball represents the earth. The smaller ball represents the moon, which has a diameter that is a bit more than one quarter of the earth's diameter. Since the earth and moon are about 30 earth diameters apart, the stick should be 1.5 m (60 in or 5 ft) long. In that way, the earth and moon part of the model will be to scale. [If you prefer, you can cut the scale in half by using a stick 0.75 m (30 in or 2.5 ft) long and spheres that are 2.5 cm (1 in) and 0.6 cm (0.25 in) in diameter, respectively.]

For a sun, you can use the real sun. It is very much out of scale for the rest of the model, but the light rays from the sun are almost parallel anyway. Hold the stick so the earth is closest to the sun, as shown in Figure 15. Tip and turn the stick until the sun, earth and moon are in line. When they are, the earth's shadow will fall on the moon. Turn the

FIGURE 15

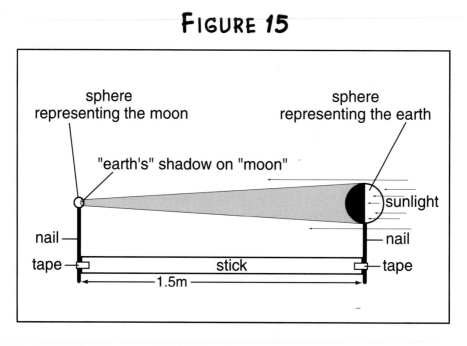

A model of a lunar eclipse is shown. The "earth," "moon," and their separation are to scale.

stick slightly in a horizontal direction. You can see the moon move into and out of the earth's shadow.

If you look closely, you can see that the earth's shadow on the moon is curved. It was the earth's curved shadow on the moon that led Greek astronomers to believe that the earth was a sphere (a ball).

But, soft! what light through yonder
window breaks?
It is the east, and Juliet is the sun!
(William Shakespeare)

3

SUN AND DIRECTION

For hikers, canoeists, boaters, and other travelers, the sun is more than a source of light and energy. It can also indicate direction. The sun's position or the direction of the shadows it casts, can help you find a direction—north, south, east, or west. If you know one direction, you can find the others. After doing the experiments in this chapter, you will be able to use the sun to find direction.

SUNRISE, SUNSET, AND DIRECTION

To do this experiment you will need:

✔ chalk

✔ notebook

✔ pen or pencil

✔ magnetic compass

To see one way the sun can be used to find direction, watch to see where it rises tomorrow morning or the next clear morning. Also watch to see where it sets tonight or on the next clear evening. **NEVER LOOK DIRECTLY AT THE SUN WHEN IT IS ABOVE THE HORIZON. IT CAN DAMAGE YOUR EYES!**

Watch for the sunrise and sunset each month over the course of a year. Choose a point where you can see the rising sun clearly. Use a piece of chalk to mark the point where you stand to watch the sunrise. If possible, choose the same point to watch both sunrise and sunset. Stand in that same place each time you watch the sun rise or set. In a notebook, record the position that you see the sun on the horizon as it rises. In the same notebook, record the place where you see the sun set on the horizon. Your record for the first day of this experiment might look like the one below. If you wish, you might also record the time of sunrise and sunset as well.

————————— ☼ —————————

Date	Me	Sunrise	Me	Sunset
Sept. 10	At center of entrance to garage (X marks the spot)	Just left of big pine tree in Mrs. Jones's yard	At center of entrance to garage (X marks the spot)	Behind Mrs. Smith's house

To make a rough estimate of the sun's direction at sunset and sunrise, hold a compass at the place or places where you watched the sun rise and set. Be sure to hold the compass away from metals such as a belt buckle. If it is working properly, the compass needle will point in a northerly direction. But it is not likely to point to true north. That is, it probably will not point toward the North Pole. The North Pole is almost directly beneath the North Star. In what general direction did the sun rise? In what general direction did the sun set?

Repeat this experiment on about the 20th of each month for at least a year. Always stand in the same place to watch each sunrise and each sunset. Does the sun rise in the same place on the horizon every day? Does the sun set at the same place on the horizon every day?

Experiment 3.2

FINDING DIRECTION WITH SUN AND WATCH

To do this experiment you will need:

✔ watch   ✔ compass
✔ sun

To make a rough estimate of direction, you can use your watch. Just point the hour hand at the sun. **REMEMBER! DO NOT LOOK DIRECTLY AT THE SUN!** South is approximately halfway between the hour hand and the number 12 on your watch (see Figure 16). The opposite direction is north.

This method assumes you are on standard time. If you are on daylight saving time, choose an hour mark one less than the time on your watch. Point that hour line at the sun.

Compare south according to your watch with the south you find using a compass. How do the directions compare? Which do you think is more accurate?

FIGURE *16*

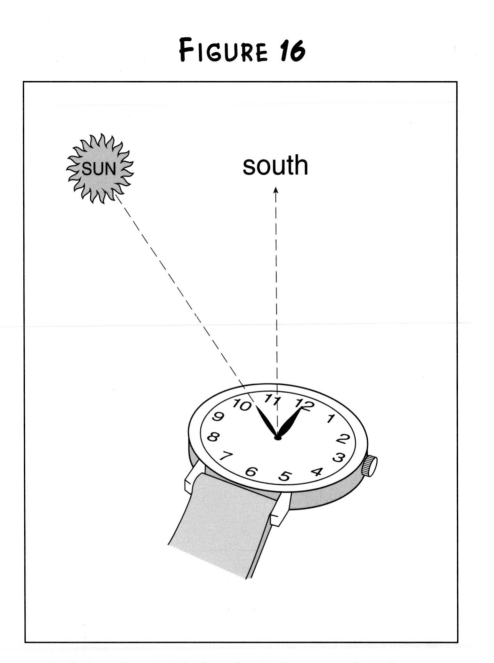

To find south, point the hour hand of your watch at the sun. South is approximately halfway between your watch's hour hand and 12 on the watch dial.

Experiment *3.3

FINDING NORTH WITH SUN AND STICK

To do this experiment you will need:

- ✔ flat open area where you can draw lines on the ground
- ✔ local daily newspaper
- ✔ stick, 30 or 60 cm (1 or 2 ft) long
- ✔ string
- ✔ large nail
- ✔ small stones
- ✔ sun
- ✔ meterstick or yardstick

You can determine the direction of north very accurately, using a stick and the sun. You will need a flat open area where you can draw lines on the ground. If possible, find a place near where you were watching the sun rise or set while you were doing Experiment 3.1. A local daily newspaper can be used to find the approximate time of midday. Most newspapers give the time of sunrise and sunset for the city or town where the paper is published. Midday at that location will occur midway between the time of sunrise and sunset. If you live close to the place where the newspaper is published, you can easily find the approximate time of midday. Just find the total time between sunrise and sunset (the paper may give that information as the length of the day) and divide it by 2. Add that time to the time of sunrise to find midday. For example, if sunrise is at 6:21 A.M. and sunset is 5:31 P.M., the total length of the day is 5 hours and 39 minutes (6:21 A.M. to 12:00 P.M.) plus 5 hours and 31 minutes (12:00 P.M. to 5:31 P.M.), which equals 10 hours and 70 minutes or 11 hours and 10 minutes. Half of 11 hours and 10 minutes is 5 and 1/2 hours + 5 minutes or 5 hours and 35 minutes. The approximate time of midday then will be the time of sunrise plus 5 hours and 35 minutes or 6:21 A.M. + 5:35 = 11:56 A.M. Midday would be expected at four minutes before noon.

About half an hour before the time of midday, push a stick into the ground. The stick should be straight up and down (vertical). Tie a loop at one end of a string. Slide the loop over and to the bottom of the vertical stick. Hold the other end of the string firmly against the base of a big nail that you will use to draw a circle on the ground. Use the length of the stick's shadow as the radius of the circle. Mark the spot where the end of the shadow touches the circle with a small stone or make an X on

FIGURE 17

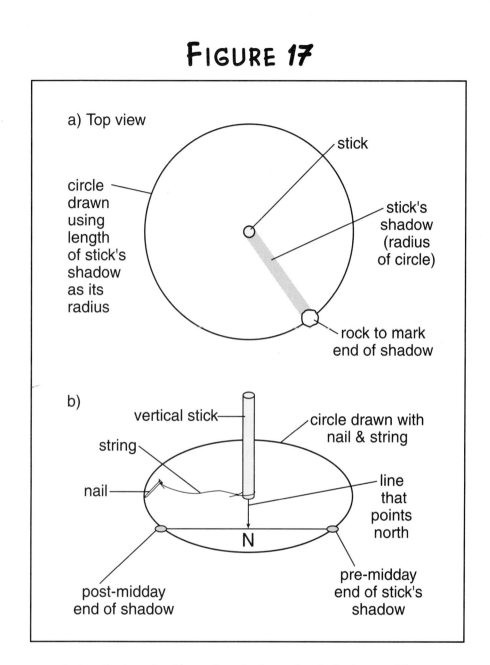

a) Top view

stick

circle drawn using length of stick's shadow as its radius

stick's shadow (radius of circle)

rock to mark end of shadow

b)

vertical stick

circle drawn with nail & string

string

nail

line that points north

N

post-midday end of shadow

pre-midday end of stick's shadow

a) Use the length of a stick's shadow, shortly before midday, as the radius of a circle about the stick. Mark the end of the shadow on the circle.

b) Mark the end of the shadow again when it touches the circle after midday. Draw a straight line connecting the two marks. A line from the stick to the center of the line you drew will point due north.

the circle at that point. Draw a circle on the ground with the nail, keeping the string tight as you travel around the stick (see Figure 17a).

As midday approaches, you will see the shadow grow shorter and shorter. After midday, it will continue to move but grow longer again. When the shadow again touches the circle, mark that spot with another small stone or an X. Draw a straight line connecting the two small stones or Xs. The line is called a chord of the circle. Using a meterstick or yardstick, mark the middle of the chord you just drew. Then draw another line from the bottom of the stick to the midpoint of the chord you just marked. The line from the stick to the midpoint of the chord will point toward true north (see Figure 17b).

Draw an arrowhead where the line ends on the chord. You have drawn an arrow that points to true north. Label it with an N. An arrowhead at the other end of the line would point due south. The stick's shortest shadow (its midday shadow) lies on the north-south line you drew.

The north-south line you have drawn can be used to find east and west too. Stand over the line and face north. Raise your right arm and extend your index finger. It will point east.

Raise your left arm in the same way. Your left index finger will point west.

To make an east-west line on the ground, simply scratch a line perpendicular to (straight across) the north-south line, as shown in Figure 18. You can label the ends of this line E (east) and W (west).

If possible, make the north-south and east-west lines more permanent. You might fill the lines on the ground with small stones or stretch heavy string between sticks driven into the ground at the ends of the two lines.

FIGURE 18

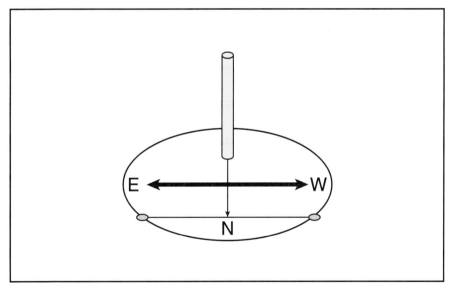

To make an east-west line simply draw a line perpendicular to the north-south line you drew earlier. Label the ends of the line E and W.

Experiment 3.4

CHECKING YOUR EAST-WEST LINE

To do this experiment you will need:

✔ **east-west line you drew on the ground in Experiment 3.3**

Before you do this experiment, you should have done Experiment 3.3. You should also have done Experiment 3.1 long enough to know that the sun does not always rise or set in the same place each day. But there are two days of the year when the sun rises due east of you and sets due west of you. On those two days, the sun is directly above the earth's equator. If you were standing on the equator, the sun would pass over the top of your head at midday. The two days on which this happens are the spring (vernal) and fall (autumnal) equinoxes. The spring equinox occurs on or about March 21, and the fall equinox takes place on or about September 22.

To check the east-west line you drew in Experiment 3.3, stand on the west end of that line just before sunrise on or near the time of an equinox. If the line you drew is accurate, the sun should rise along the extension of your east line. On the same day, the sun should set along the extension of the west line you drew. Did the sun rise and set in the east and west according to the line you made in Experiment 3.3?

Experiment *3.5

SUN, SNOW, AND DIRECTION

To do this experiment you will need:

✔ snow

✔ sun

✔ old, cut corn stalks in a field

If you live in a region where it snows, you can often tell direction by looking at the patterns of melting snow. Would you expect snow to melt faster on the north or south side of a mound or hill? Why?

Could the ground on the south side of a house be bare while the ground on the north side remains snow-covered?

If you live in the country, look closely at snow melting around old, cut corn stalks. Can you explain why the melted-snow holes around the stalks are larger and less steep on the north side of the stalks?

What other snow patterns can you find that could be used to indicate direction?

*To him whose elastic and vigorous thought
keeps pace with the sun,
the day is a perpetual morning.
(Henry David Thoreau)*

4

SUN AND TIME

From your experiments in Chapter 3, you know that the sun moves from an easterly to a westerly direction each day. As it moves, the shadows it casts change. They change both in length and direction. Early Egyptians used a stick's changing shadow to make a clock. The direction that we call clockwise (the direction that the hands of a clock move) probably came from the movement of a shadow clock's hand. In fact, the earliest clocks were less accurate than the sundials that were used to set them.

Experiment *4.1

A SHADOW CLOCK

To do this experiment you will need:

- ✔ wooden board or a sheet of cardboard about 30 cm (12 in) on a side
- ✔ finishing nail 5–8 cm (2–3 in long)
- ✔ hammer
- ✔ scissors
- ✔ sheet of paper
- ✔ tape
- ✔ sunny, level place outdoors
- ✔ stones (if cardboard is used)
- ✔ pencil
- ✔ watch

Find a board or a sheet of cardboard about 30 cm (12 in) on a side and a finishing nail 5–8 cm (2–3 in) long. Use a hammer to drive the nail a short distance into the board or push it into the cardboard. The nail should be near the middle of one end of the board, about 5 cm (2 in) from the edge (see Figure 19a).

Use scissors to make a 5-cm (2-in) slit at the edge of the center of the long side of a sheet of paper. The slit allows you to slide the paper past the upright nail. Tape the paper to the wood or cardboard and put it in a sunny, level place outdoors, shortly after sunrise. If you use

FIGURE 19

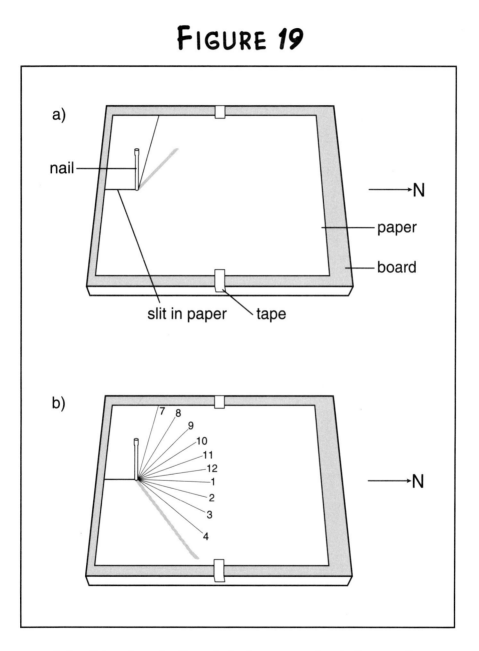

a) A nail in a board will cast shadows on a sheet of paper. Draw lines along the nail's shadow at different times.

b) Label the lines with the times at which you drew them.

a cardboard base, put stones on its corners to hold it in place. Be sure the nail is on the south side of the paper.

Use a pencil to mark the position of the nail's shadow on the paper at one-hour intervals throughout the day. Label each line you draw with the time you read on a watch, as shown in Figure 19b.

Mark the position of the board so you can put it in exactly the same place several days, weeks, or months later. Compare the times on the shadow clock with times on your watch during a day several days after you make the shadow clock. Do the same thing a week later. Do it again a month later. Do the times on your shadow clock still agree with the times on your clock or watch after several days? after a week? after a month? Do you think the Egyptian shadow clock was a very accurate timepiece? Do you think they cared? How do you think they measured time at night?

Experiment *4.2

A SUNDIAL

To do this experiment you will need:

- ✔ good map of your local area
- ✔ an ADULT
- ✔ board about 15 cm x 15 cm x 2 cm (6 in x 6 in x 3/4 in) to make a gnomon
- ✔ piece of plywood about 30 cm x 30 cm (12 in x 12 in) to make base for gnomon
- ✔ glue
- ✔ blocks and/or clamps
- ✔ pencil
- ✔ sunny, level place outdoors
- ✔ watch
- ✔ pen and ruler
- ✔ protractor

At some point in time, someone discovered that a more accurate timepiece could be made by tipping the stick on a shadow clock. If the angle between the stick and the ground is equal to the latitude, the shadow cast by the stick is a more accurate indicator of time. Rather than a stick, many sundials have a vertical plate, called a gnomon. The gnomon is set vertically on a base plate. It is cut so that the angle it makes with the base plate equals the latitude where the sundial is to be placed. For example, on Cape Cod, Massachusetts at a latitude of 41.5 degrees the gnomon should be cut to make an angle of 41.5 degrees with the base to which it is attached (see Figure 20).

To see if a sundial is a better timepiece than a shadow clock, you can make your own sundial. First, use a good map to find the latitude where you live. Then **ASK AN ADULT** to cut a board with an angle equal to the latitude where you live. That board will be your gnomon. Glue it to another board that will serve as the base. Support the gnomon with blocks or clamps. It should stand vertically on the base until the glue dries. If

FIGURE 20

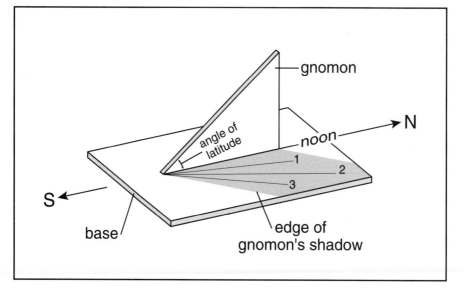

The gnomon on a sundial should be cut at an angle equal to the latitude where it will be located.

you sight along a properly cut and oriented gnomon, it will point toward the North Star.

At midday, if the sun is shining, place the base and gnomon on a level surface in bright sunlight. Turn the base until the gnomon casts no shadow to either side. At midday, the only shadow should point due north in line with the gnomon. Mark the center of this shadow with a pencil and label it noon. By how many minutes does midday noon according to the sun differ from 12:00 P.M. on your watch?

Exactly one hour later, use the pencil to mark the edge of the gnomon's shadow on its east side. (With the sun to the west of midday, the gnomon's shadow will fall on the east side of the base.) Label this line 1. Continue to mark and label the edge of the gnomon's shadow at one-hour intervals until sunset. Of course the lines may not agree with your watch unless midday according to the sun happened to occur at noon according to the clock.

Once you have marked the afternoon hours, you can use a protractor and pencil to mark the morning hours. For example, 11:00 A.M. will lie along a line that makes the same angle on the west side of the gnomon as 1:00 P.M. did on the east side in the afternoon. Similarly, 10:00 A.M. will be at the same angle as 2:00 P.M., 9:00 A.M. will correspond to 3:00 P.M., and so on.

Once you have marked the hour lines with a pencil, you can use a ruler and a pen with dark ink to make permanent hour lines on the base. Try to keep the sundial in the same place over the course of a year. Is the sundial you have made a more accurate timepiece than the shadow clock? Does it keep perfect time?

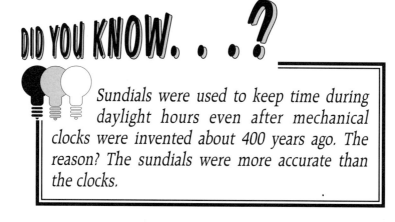

DID YOU KNOW. . .?

Sundials were used to keep time during daylight hours even after mechanical clocks were invented about 400 years ago. The reason? The sundials were more accurate than the clocks.

Experiment 4.3

MAPPING THE SUN'S PATH ACROSS THE SKY

To do this experiment you will need:

- ✔ clear plastic dome or fine-mesh kitchen strainer
- ✔ cardboard
- ✔ pencil
- ✔ ruler
- ✔ tape
- ✔ sunny, level surface outdoors
- ✔ marking pen or round-headed pins or small pieces of masking tape
- ✔ calendar

You know that during the course of a day the sun moves from east to west, but what is its path across the sky? You can map the sun's path by using a clear plastic dome or a fine-mesh kitchen strainer to represent the sky. Astronomers call the sky the celestial hemisphere (half a giant ball). If you think about it, the sky does resemble a hemisphere. Of course, we see only half the sky at any one time. The other half is blocked out by the earth. Twelve hours later, we can see the other hemisphere. The total sky (the sky surrounding the entire globe) is called the celestial sphere.

To map the sun's path across the celestial hemisphere, place the dome or strainer on a sheet of cardboard. Use a pencil to mark the edge of the dome or strainer on the cardboard, as shown in Figure 21a. Remove the dome or strainer and use a ruler and the pencil to make a small solid circle (dot) at the center of the circle you drew on the cardboard. Then put the dome or strainer back in its original position and tape it to the cardboard.

Shortly after sunrise, place the dome or strainer outside on a level surface that will be bathed in sunlight all day. Mark the position of the cardboard so you can put it back in the same place if it should be moved accidentally.

If you are using a clear plastic dome, you can mark the sun's path across the sky with a marking pen. Place the tip of the pen on the dome so that the shadow of the pen tip falls on the small solid circle you drew at the center of the dome (Figure 21b). Mark that point on the dome. That point on the dome corresponds to the sun's place on the celestial hemisphere. It is in line with the sun and the small circle on the cardboard. The small circle represents your position at the center of the celestial hemisphere.

FIGURE 21

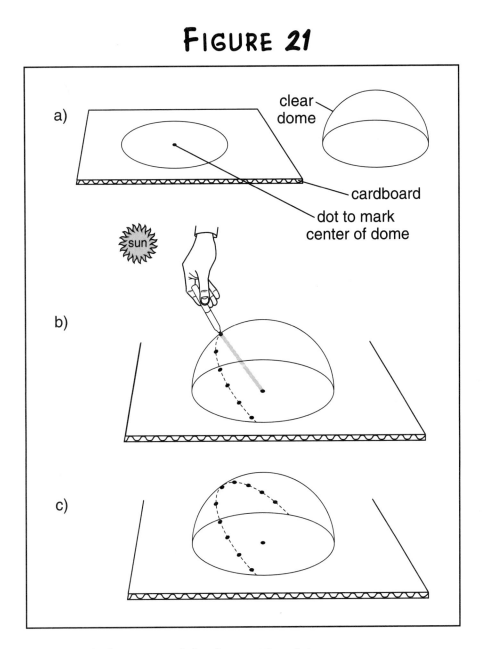

a) Mark the center of the dome with a dot.

b) Use a marking pen to map the sun's position in the sky. The shadow of the pen's tip should fall on the dot at the center of the dome.

c) By the end of the day, you will have a map of the sun's path.

If you use a strainer, round-headed pins or small pieces of masking tape can be used to cast shadows on the small, solid circle.

Continue to mark the sun's position on the dome or strainer as often as you can throughout the day. Together, all the marks, pins, or pieces of tape will make a map of the sun's path across the sky (see Figure 21c). If you used a strainer, connect the pins or pieces of tape with a piece of colored yarn so that you will have a permanent map of the sun's path.

Repeat this experiment at different times of the year. If possible, try to map the sun on or about the 20th of June, September, December, and March. Different colored marks can be used to identify the date you did the experiment if you have only one dome.

These maps of the sun's path will help you to confirm or answer a number of questions. For example: Does the sun rise and set in the same place every day? Does the sun's path across the sky change over the course of a year? Does the sun's midday altitude change?

How can you use the maps you have made to determine the direction of sunrise and sunset at different times of the year? How can you use the maps to determine the sun's midday altitude at different times of the year?

Experiment 4.4

MIDDAY BY SHORTEST SHADOW

To do this experiment you will need:

- ✔ stick, 30 or 60 cm (1 or 2 ft) long
- ✔ meterstick or yardstick
- ✔ watch
- ✔ pencil and paper

In Experiment 3.3, you found true north by finding a stick's shortest shadow. An object's shortest shadow may or may not occur at noon, according to a clock. The sun casts the day's shortest shadows when it is due south of the ground it illuminates. This is midday according to the sun. The sun knows nothing about the time on your watch or clock. If you live near the eastern end of a time zone, midday may occur an hour earlier than it does at the western end of the time zone.

Does the time of midday according to the sun always occur at the same time according to a clock? To find out, use a meterstick or a yardstick to measure a stick's shortest (midday) shadow at different times of the year.

Be sure to set your watch according to the radio each time you do the experiment.

You will have to measure the stick's shadow frequently (every minute) at times close to midday. (You can approximate the time of midday using the same method you used in Experiment 3.3.) Record the lengths and times. Once the shadow begins to lengthen, you will know midday has past. You can then record the time at which the shortest shadow appeared. You may be surprised to find that midday according to the sun may vary by as much as thirty minutes according to the clock.

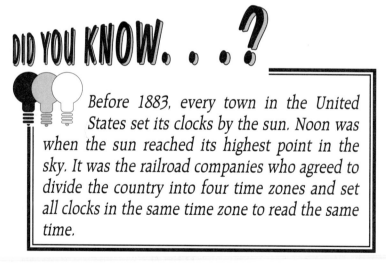

DID YOU KNOW. . .?

Before 1883, every town in the United States set its clocks by the sun. Noon was when the sun reached its highest point in the sky. It was the railroad companies who agreed to divide the country into four time zones and set all clocks in the same time zone to read the same time.

Experiment *4.5

CHANGING LENGTHS OF DAY

To do this experiment you will need:

- ✔ daily newspaper
- ✔ pen or pencil
- ✔ notebook

From Experiment 3.3, you know that the time of midday can be found by determining the midpoint in time between sunrise and sunset. You know, too, from your observations of the sun that the total hours of daylight increase between the first day of winter (about December 20) and the first day of summer (about June 20). The hours of daylight decrease from June 20 to December 20. But do these hours of daylight increase or decrease equally at both ends of the day?

You can investigate this question quite easily using a newspaper. Make a daily record of the time of sunrise, sunset, and total length of daylight over the course of a year. Be sure to record this information from late December to late January when it is particularly interesting.

A sample portion of such a record is shown below.

	SUNRISE		SUNSET		LENGTH OF DAY	
DATE	hr	min	hr	min	hr	min
7/1	4	11	7	25	15	14
7/2	4	12	7	25	15	13
7/3	4	12	7	24	15	12

After you have collected your data, study it carefully. Do the hours of daylight grow longer or shorter by equal amounts at both ends of the day during the course of a year? If not, when during the year does the day grow longer or shorter because of changes in the time of sunset? When does the day grow longer or shorter because of changes in the time of sunrise?

Fear no more the heat o' the sun.
(William Shakespeare)

5

Sun and Energy

Although the earth's center is very hot (approximately 6,500°C or 12,000°F), our only source of external heat is the sun. It is also our only source of natural light other than the dim light we receive from other stars. Without the sun we would not have enough light or heat and nothing could live on the earth.

Experiment *5.1

ABSORBING SOLAR ENERGY

To do this experiment you will need:

- ✔ two small shiny tin cans
- ✔ flat black paint
- ✔ paintbrush
- ✔ cold water
- ✔ thermometer
- ✔ small sheet of cardboard
- ✔ bright sunshine
- ✔ watch

If you stand in bright sunlight on a calm day, you can feel the sun's heat. You may have noticed the sense of warmth is particularly noticeable if you are wearing dark clothes.

To see how color affects the absorption of the sun's energy, you will need two small, shiny tin cans. Paint one of the cans black. Use a flat black paint. Apply paint to both the inside and outside of the can. When the paint has dried, half fill both cans with equal amounts of cold water. Use a thermometer to determine the temperature of the water in the two cans. It should be the same for both.

Put both cans side by side on a sheet of cardboard in bright sunlight where the temperature is greater than the temperature of the water. A sunny window would be appropriate in the winter; a bright patch of ground would be satisfactory in warm weather. After an hour, determine the temperature of the water in both cans. Continue to measure the temperature of the water in the two cans at one-hour intervals. In which can does the temperature change the most? How does color affect the absorption of solar energy?

DID YOU KNOW. . .?

Light can enter your eyes even when your eyes are closed. To see that this is true, turn your head toward a ceiling light, close your eyes, and turn the light on and off.

Experiment 5.2

REFLECTING SUNLIGHT

To do this experiment you will need:

- ✔ two mirrors
- ✔ a friend
- ✔ rural area
- ✔ Morse code
- ✔ sun

In the previous experiment, you found that water in the shiny container absorbed less heat than the water in the dark one. The shiny container reflected much of the sunlight. A mirror will reflect almost all of the sunlight that strikes it. Hold a mirror in sunlight and reflect the light onto a building or the ground. **BE CAREFUL! DO NOT REFLECT THE SUNLIGHT INTO ANYONE'S EYES!** You will find that the mirror does not grow noticeably warmer.

You can use a mirror to send messages by reflecting sunlight. If possible, have a friend stand about 100 m (330 ft) from you. Two hilltops would be ideal, but any open space can be used. Reflect the sunlight from your mirror so that it briefly strikes your friend. You will find that the light beam reflected from a mirror becomes circular and grows larger as the distance from the mirror increases. Once you are able to reflect light to your partner, you can send messages by Morse code. A brief reflected pulse of light can represent a dot. A slightly longer pulse of light can be used to represent a dash. Then, using the code shown in Figure 22, you can flash messages to your friend. He or she can flash messages back to you using the same code.

FIGURE 22

A) · —	N) — ·	1) · — — — —
B) — · · ·	O) — — —	2) · · — — —
C) — · — ·	P) · — — ·	3) · · · — —
D) — · ·	Q) — — · —	4) · · · · —
E) ·	R) · — ·	5) · · · · ·
F) · · — ·	S) · · ·	6) — · · · ·
G) — — ·	T) —	7) — — · · ·
H) · · · ·	U) · · —	8) — — — · ·
I) · ·	V) · · · —	9) — — — — ·
J) · — — —	W) · — —	0) — — — — —
K) — · —	X) — · · —	,) — — · · — —
L) · — · ·	Y) — · — —	.) · — · — · —
M) — —	Z) — — · ·	?) · · — — · ·

The Morse code, which was used in telegraphy, can also be used for signaling with flashes of light or waves of a flag. In addition to letters, the code allows a sender to transmit numbers and punctuation as well.

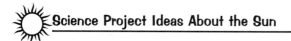

Experiment *5.3

FOCUSED SUNLIGHT

To do this experiment you will need:

✔ an ADULT

✔ magnifying glass or concave mirror such as a shaving or makeup mirror

✔ piece of paper

✔ bright sunlight

A power plant in Odeillo, Font-Romeu, France intensifies the heat from the sun. The power plant uses sixty-three large mirrors to reflect light onto a large curved mirror. The curved mirror focuses the sunlight onto a dark tank that contains water (see Figure 23). The intense light striking the tank causes the water to boil. Steam emerging from the tank under pressure is used to turn a generator that produces electricity.

To see how sunlight can be brought together to increase its intensity, **ASK AN ADULT** to help you. Have the adult hold a small piece of paper in bright sunlight while you hold a magnifying glass (lens) about 6 cm (2 in) from the paper. The lens will bend the

FIGURE 23

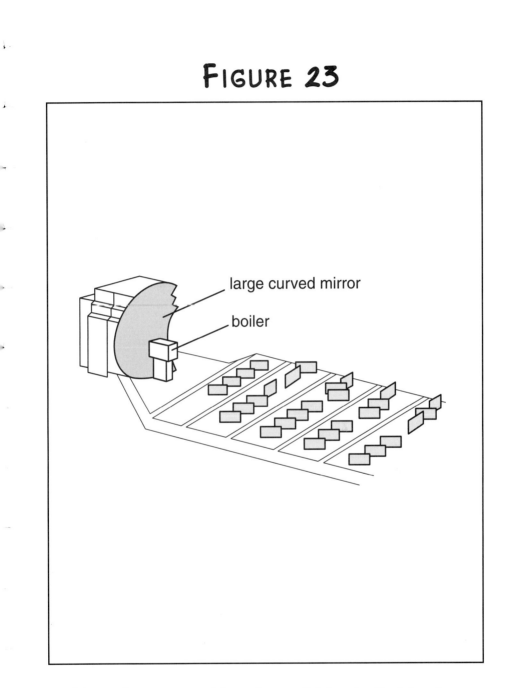

Many mirrors are used to gather sunlight and reflect it onto a large curved mirror. The curved mirror focuses the light onto a small area so that the light becomes very intense. It is so intense that it can make water boil, producing steam that can be used to generate electricity.

sunlight and bring the light rays together to make the light more intense. (If you have a concave mirror, such as a shaving or makeup mirror, you can focus the sunlight with the mirror.) Move the lens back and forth until the spot of light on the paper is as small as you can possibly make it. You will see the paper begin to smoke because it is so hot where the light has been brought together by the lens (or concave mirror).

Now turn the lens (or mirror) slightly so that the spot of light is spread over a larger area. Does the paper continue to smoke? Stop the experiment before the paper catches fire.

In Experiment 1.2 you saw how the intensity of sunlight striking the earth is affected by the season. How is the experiment you have just done similar to Experiment 1.2?

DID YOU KNOW. . .?

Sunlight can be changed directly to electrical energy by letting the sun shine on photovoltaic cells. These cells convert light to electrical energy. You may have seen clusters of photovoltaic cells on remote buildings that are not connected to a power line, or on pocket calculators that work only in light.

Experiment *5.4

SUN, PLANTS, AND LIFE

To do this experiment you will need:

- ✔ green grass
- ✔ small board or flat stone
- ✔ bean or corn seeds
- ✔ two flower pots
- ✔ potting soil
- ✔ warm dark place
- ✔ warm sunny place
- ✔ water
- ✔ sunflower seeds
- ✔ soil

Sunlight is the source of the energy found in the food we eat. Therefore, sunlight is essential to life because we cannot live without food. In the presence of sunlight, green plants can manufacture food. Chlorophyll, the pigment that gives green plants their color, enables these plants to chemically combine carbon dioxide and water to form food (sugars and starches) and oxygen. Energy is stored in that food. The energy comes from sunlight that is captured by chlorophyll when the plants manufacture food. The oxygen that is also a product of this process is the oxygen found in the air we breathe.

To see what happens to green plants when light is not present, ask permission to place a small board or flat stone on some green grass. Choose a spot where the board will not be disturbed. Look at the grass under the board every few days. What happens to the color of the grass? When the grass is almost white, remove the board. Continue to look at the grass every few days. Does the grass become green again? Do you think light is needed for plants to make chlorophyll?

Here is another experiment you can do to see the effect of darkness on green plants. Plant some bean or corn seeds about 1 cm (0.5 in) deep in two separate pots filled with potting soil. Put one of the pots in a warm dark place. Put the other pot in a warm sunny place. Keep the soil in both pots damp but not wet.

Allow a week or two for the seeds to sprout. Will the seeds sprout in darkness? Will the seeds sprout in sunlight? If they sprout, how long will the plants continue to grow in darkness? How long will they continue to grow in sunlight? What is different about the plants that are in darkness?

It might be fun to grow some sunflowers. Plant some sunflower seeds in a row early in the summer. Follow the directions on the package that the seeds come in. Water the seeds frequently if it doesn't rain. It will take several weeks for the seeds to sprout and emerge from the soil. Continue to water the plants if the soil becomes dry.

The plants may grow to be taller than you before their giant flowers appear. Why do you think they are called sunflowers?

When the backs of the flowers turn yellow in late summer, you can cut off the flowers and hang them in a cool place for several weeks. After that you can gather the seeds. If you crack open the outer shell of a sunflower seed, you will find the inner softer part to be very tasty.

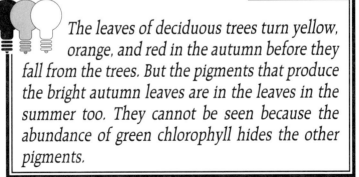

DID YOU KNOW. . .?

The leaves of deciduous trees turn yellow, orange, and red in the autumn before they fall from the trees. But the pigments that produce the bright autumn leaves are in the leaves in the summer too. They cannot be seen because the abundance of green chlorophyll hides the other pigments.

Experiment *5.5

SOLAR ENERGY

To do this experiment you will need:

- ✔ cardboard box about 30 cm X 20 cm x 10 cm (12 in x 8 in x 4 in)
- ✔ scissors
- ✔ newspaper
- ✔ large nail
- ✔ two small plastic funnels
- ✔ ruler
- ✔ sheet of cardboard
- ✔ heavy-duty aluminum foil
- ✔ flat black paint
- ✔ paintbrush
- ✔ tape
- ✔ giant 8-mm (5/16-in) diameter drinking straw or plastic tube
- ✔ thick pin
- ✔ clay
- ✔ short length of plastic or rubber tubing
- ✔ clear plasic wrap
- ✔ water
- ✔ two small cups
- ✔ thermometer

Many homes and other buildings use the sun to heat water and interior space. Some homes use passive solar heating in which the sun's energy is absorbed by large masses of dark concrete or large dark barrels filled with water. At night, as outside air temperatures fall, the heat stored in the water or concrete is used to warm the air inside the building.

Other homes use active solar heating. This involves pumping water to solar collectors that are usually located on the south-facing roof of the building. Each collector has a transparent glass or plastic cover that allows sunlight to enter. Under the cover is a dark surface with coils through which water circulates. The water is warmed by the sunlight and passes to a storage tank where it may be used to heat the building or to heat water for baths, showers, and washing clothes and dishes. On cloudy days, the water can be heated by a furnace.

You can build a small model of a solar collector to see how it works. The frame of your model collector can be a cardboard box about 30 cm long, 20 cm wide, and 10 cm deep (12 in x 8 in x 4 in). Cut the flaps off the box and fill the bottom half with crumpled newspaper. The paper acts as an insulator. Use a large nail to make a hole near one corner of the box, as shown in Figure 24. The hole should be about 5 cm (2 in) in from one side and halfway down the side of what will be the lower end of the collector. The hole is used to support the spout of a plastic funnel that will collect water that flows along the collector.

Measure the distance from the top of the box to the top of the funnel. Cut a sheet of cardboard equal to that length. Its width should be the inside width of the box. Be sure the cardboard fits tightly so that it holds the funnel in place.

Next, cut a piece of heavy-duty aluminum foil 5 cm (2 in) wider than the box with a length that matches the box. Paint the foil with a flat black paint.

When the paint is dry, lay the foil on the cardboard. Center the foil, fold the extra few centimeters (about an inch) on each side against the box, and tape it in place. Turn the edge of the foil at the funnel end of the box so that it forms a trough that will carry water to the funnel. Use the nail again to punch a hole in the foil so water will be able to run into the funnel.

Take a giant 8-mm (5/16-in) diameter drinking straw or plastic tube and use a thick pin to make six to eight holes along a straight line on one side of the straw. Plug one end of the straw or tube with clay. Then tape it to the aluminum foil near the top of the box, as shown in Figure 24. Use the large nail to punch another hole through the side of the box so that the open end of the straw or tube can be connected to another funnel with a short length of plastic or rubber tubing.

Finally, cover the open top of the box with clear plastic wrap. Tape the edges of the wrap to the sides of the box. Your model collector is now ready to heat water.

FIGURE 24

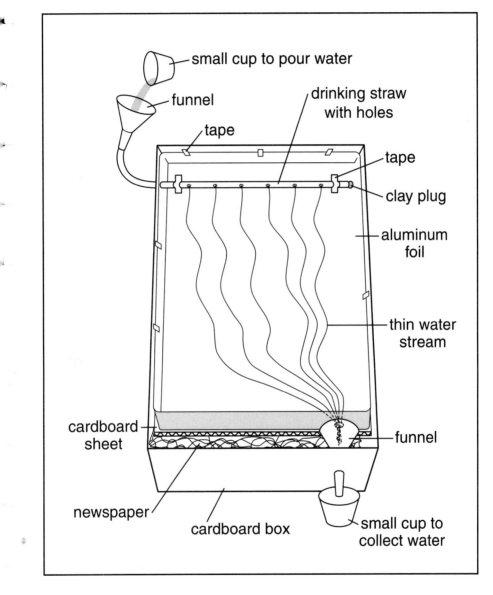

small cup to pour water

funnel

drinking straw
with holes

tape

tape

clay plug

aluminum
foil

thin water
stream

cardboard
sheet

funnel

newspaper

cardboard box

small cup to
collect water

You can make a model of a solar collector.

Place the collector in a sunny place with the black aluminum foil facing the sun. Tip the box so that the end with the straw or tube is slightly higher than the other end where the water will be collected. Use a thermometer to find the temperature of 50 ml (2 oz) of cold water in a small cup. Place another small cup under the end of the funnel at the lower end of the collector. Then slowly pour the water into the funnel at the upper end of the box. Watch the water flow out the holes in the straw or tube and down the aluminum foil to the trough where it flows into the other funnel and out into the small cup.

Remove the cup of water and replace it with the empty cup that first held the cold water. Pour the water you just collected back into the upper funnel so it can flow over the dark aluminum foil again. (In a real collector a pump would circulate water from the collector to a storage tank and back to the collector.) Repeat this procedure five or six times. Then measure the temperature of the water that has circulated through the collector. How much has the water temperature increased? How warm can you make the water if you let it flow through the collector many times? Can you find ways to make your model collector more efficient?

ANSWERS

CHAPTER 1 *(P. 12):*

1) 4

2) 4 sq cm

3) 24 sq cm

4) It is 4 times as large (24 sq cm vs. 6 sq cm).

5) 8 times

6) 8 cu cm

7) They are the same.

CHAPTER 2 *(MYSTERY SHADOWS, PP. 24–25):*

a) A basketball hoop and backboard.

b) The Gateway Arch in Saint Louis, Missouri.

c) A backhoe (see photo 1 below).

d) An opening in the wall of a church (see photo 2 below).

e) A man carrying a canoe (see photo 3 below).

(1)

(2)

(3)

FURTHER READING

Ardley, Neil. *Sun and Light*. New York: Watts, 1983.

Arnold, Caroline. *Sun Fun*. New York: Watts, 1981.

Asimov, Isaac. *The Sun*. Milwaukee: G. Stevens, 1988.

———. *How Did We Find Out About Sunshine*. New York: Walker, 1987.

Bendick, Jeanne. *The Sun: Our Very Own Star*. Brookfield, Conn.: Millbrook, 1991.

Daily, Bob. *The Sun*. New York: Watts, 1994.

Gardner, Robert. *Projects in Space Science*. New York: Messner, 1988.

Gardner, Robert and David Webster. *Science in Your Backyard*. New York: Messner, 1987.

Jaber, Willima. *Exploring the Sun*. New York: Messner, 1980.

Simon, Seymour. *The Sun*. New York: Morrow, 1986.

Zim, Herbert S. *The Sun*. New York: Morrow, 1975.

LIST OF MATERIALS

A
aluminum foil, heavy-duty

B
ball
blocks
board, small
board, wooden
box, cardboard
box, small

C
calendar
cans, small shiny tin
cardboard
chalk
clamps
clay
compass, magnetic
cone-shaped object
corn stalks, old
cups, small

D
dome, clear plastic

drinking straw

F
file cards
flashlight
flower pots
funnels, small plastic

G
globe
glue
grass, green

H
hammer

L
lamp socket
lightbulb
local map

M
magnifying glass
marking pen
masking tape
meterstick or yardstick
mirror, shaving or makeup
Morse code

N
nails
newspaper, local daily
notebook

P
paint, flat black
paintbrush
paper
pegboard
pen
pencil
penny
pins
plastic wrap, clear
plate, small
plywood
potting soil
protractor
pyramid-shaped object

R
ruler

S
scissors
seeds, bean or corn

seeds, sunflower
snow
soil
spheres, Styrofoam or other soft opaque
sticks
stones
strainer, fine-mesh kitchen
string
sunlight

T
tall post or flagpole
tape
thermometer, outdoor
tree with leaves
tubing, plastic or rubber

W
wall, white
watch
water
wooden board

INDEX